Dino Breaks The Rules

Sarah Read

Go here to get

https://BookHip.com/HQWTBQ

"The Anxious Monster" for FREE!

THIS BOOK BELONGS TO

....

....

Dino hated following rules. He didn't understand why he couldn't do what he wanted to do. Every time he tried to have fun, someone said, "Dino, don't do that." It made him grumpy. He only wanted to have fun!

One day Dino's mom told him and his sister to get ready to go to the supermarket. Dino was ready to go. He bounced up and down. Boing! Boing! Boing!

As they pulled into the parking lot, Dino was very excited. There was so much to see and so much to do. He knew he was going to have a lot of fun.

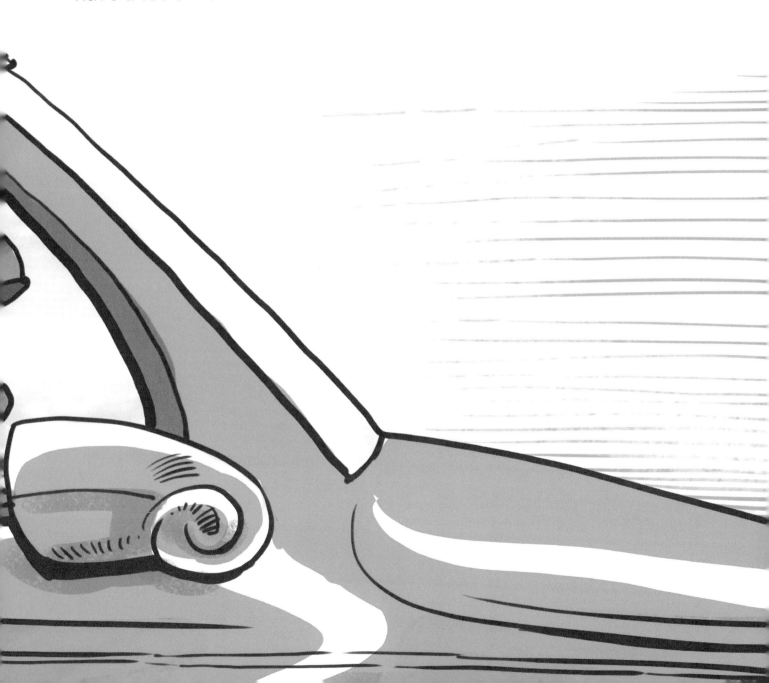

"Can I have my own cart, Mommy? Dino's little sister asked. "I want to be like you."

"If she has a cart, I want one too, Mommy." Dino yelled.

"You can both have a cart, as long as you follow the rules," Dino's mom said.

Dino was so focused on choosing a small blue cart that he didn't hear his mom's words.

Dino's little sister picked out a small pink cart and followed behind their mom. She only put the things in her cart that Mom gave her.

Dino had other ideas.

"Come on, race with me," he begged his sister.

Mom was reading the cans so didn't notice when Dino pushed his sister to get her to race. Push!

"Race with me, come on!" he said again.

He had pushed his sister a little too hard. She fell backward and crashed against the canned food pile in the aisle.

"Oh no!" Dino watched horrified as the cans fell down around his sister.

"Dino! You could have hurt your sister. Now someone has to clean up this mess."

Dino hung his head. He never meant to hurt his sister. Maybe he shouldn't run in grocery stores. Other people could get hurt. He vowed to never race in a supermarket again because he didn't want to hurt anyone.

The next day at school, Dino laughed and played with his friends. After recess, all his friends threw their empty soda cans onto the ground. Dino looked up at the "No Littering" sign.

"Well," Dino grumbled to himself, "if they don't throw their trash away, then I don't need to either.

He dropped his soda can on the ground and ran to his next class.

When the day was over, Dino was rushing to the bus stop when he suddenly slipped and fell right on his bottom!

"Ouch! That hurt," Dino exclaimed.
He looked around and saw a banana peel on the ground.

"Did I slip on that?" Dino remembered the "No Littering" sign he had ignored. He slipped on the banana because somebody hadn't thrown it away. He felt bad that he hadn't thrown his own trash away at recess.

"I should teach my friends that littering is bad." Dino said to himself.

11

The next day the teacher read the class a story.

"And what happened next?" Dino kept asking.
The other students were getting upset by his interruptions.
They couldn't hear the story.

"Now, Dino," the teacher started gently, "I know you're excited, but everyone wants to hear the story."

Dino looked around at the sad faces and felt bad. He chose to be quiet during the rest of storytime so his friends could hear the story too.

On Friday, Dino's mom waited for him at the bus stop.
He hopped off the bus and ran into her arms.

"I made you a cake, Dino," she said,
"but let's save it until after dinner when everyone can have some."

Dino ran into the house to look at the cake. It was a yummy chocolate cake with chocolate frosting. Dino's favorite. His tummy growled with hunger. Dino looked at the cake for a few seconds and then looked at his mom.

"Mom, I'm happy to wait for everyone. That would be more fun!"

While Mom started dinner, Dino ate his snack and told her all about the lessons he had learned that week.

Thank you

What Did You Think of *Dino Breaks The Rules?*

Thank you for purchasing this book. I know you could have picked any number of books to read, but you picked this book and for that I am extremely grateful.

If you like the book... and if you'd be willing to spare just two or three minutes... would you be willing to share your review of the book on Amazon?

If you would, it would mean the absolute world to me!

Thank you SO much. This helps to get the book into as many hands as possible, helping other parents and educators!

I really appreciate all your support!

Sarah Read
children's book author

Go here to get

https://BookHip.com/HQWTBQ

"The Anxious Monster" for FREE!

Made in the USA
Las Vegas, NV
25 February 2024